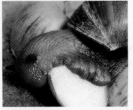

How to Care for Your

Giant African Land Snail

CONTENTS

Photos by:
Colin Jeal

KINGDOM

s, A division of Interpet

Dorking, Surrey, RH4 3YX

INTRODUCTION

As every child knows, snails are fascinating creatures. I am sure many of us spent happy childhood hours in gardens searching for beasties and filled whole jars with garden snails. Equally, I am just as sure that we were all made to put them back by our mothers, horrified at the thought of a house full of slimy things!

To those of us still yearning for 'slimy things', the Giant African land snail may just be the answer. Those most interested in the keeping of these beautiful creatures are probably children (or those of us who are still children at heart!), and the fact the snails are 'giant' makes them even more appealing. Snails can solve a few more problems for parents than might at first be believed. Although they may disgust Aunt Matilda, snails are the perfect pets for those on a limited income, if a child is allergic to fur or feathers but does not want fish or reptiles, or if the family cannot cope with dogs or cats. Snails can be easily taken on holiday (within the UK), and are ideal for smaller children (under supervision) as, apart from dropping them, there is little damage that small fingers can do to a snail.

A snail can make an inexpensive but interesting pet.

FAMILY HISTORY

Snails are part of the group of creatures known as *molusca*, or soft bodied animals. The sub-group or 'class' that snails belong to is known as *gastropod*. This literally means 'belly-footed', as a snail moves about on its belly which is referred to as the foot. This foot is usually tapered in shape. The gastropods are one of the most adaptable of all types of animals, and are found not only on land, but in fresh water and the marine environment. The most common form of marine gastropod is the nudibranch, or sea slug. The largest of all the gastropods is found in the warm seas off Australia: the *Megalatractus aruanus* grows to a shell length of 60cm.

To help them glide from place to place every gastropod produces mucus, which is why all snails and slugs are slimy. Slugs are, of course, just snails without shells.

The body of a snail consists of four main parts: visceral hump, mantle, head and foot. The body can be withdrawn into its shell.

You may think that your snail has four eyes but, in fact, it has only two. The bottom two tentacles are sensory organs which the snail uses to feel its way around, and the top two are its eyes, which have very little, if any, real sight. These upper tentacles are *invaginable*. This means that they can be rolled in and out. Watch your snail as it goes in and out of its shell and you will see its eyes rolling on stalks.

Right: 'Smile, please!' A snail's mouth contains thousands of 'teeth', which it uses to rasp at the food.

The Giant African land snail is just one of 22,000 terrestrial species which have adapted to nearly every type of environment, from deserts to snow-covered Alpine slopes.

Snails eat most things but mainly vegetation, and some are so effective that they become harmful pests, causing serious crop destruction in some parts of the world.

Snails are very useful to man. In many countries they are eaten as food and, in their native Africa, the Giant land snails are regarded as a very tasty meal. During the Second World War African land snails were introduced to many tropical places as a food source for the troops. It is in these countries that snails have become pests and in some places have caused the extinction of other snail species. This has happened in two ways: first, due to Giant land snails taking over native snails' habitats and food reserves and, second, through man's effort to put things right.

Tiny snails were introduced to the Pacific islands to eat the Giant African land snails but decided that the native *Partula* snails tasted better! This led to the extinction of at least one species of *Partula* and several others are endangered. Zoos in this country are now working together on a breeding programme which, hopefully, will lead to the reintroduction of the *Partula* snails into the wild.

You are likely to come across only two species of the Giant African land snail in captivity. These are the commonly-seen East African species *Achatina fulica* and the West African *Achatina marginata*. Both species look very similar but the East African land snail is normally smaller and has a pointed apex (top of shell), whereas the snail from the west has a rounded apex. The only other way of telling them apart is the size and number of eggs produced. The West African snail produces only about six eggs at a time, which at 15mm are big for snails, compared with the eastern species which has eggs of 3-4mm, and can lay up to several hundred at one time.

The other species of snail that has been kept in captivity is *Achatina achatina*. This is the largest of the land snails, and can grow to about 20cm. The largest recorded specimen measured 37.5cm from snout to tail, the shell length was 27cm and it weighed nearly one kilogram! This particular snail had been collected from the wild and it is unlikely that you will find one available as a pet. It is improbable, but not impossible, that you would be able to grow your pet snail as big as this, but I know plenty of people who are trying.

The snail is standing on the edge of its foot to gain height. Snails do this as part of the mating process.

BUYING

Not all pet shops stock Giant African land snails as yet. However, snails are becoming more popular and pet shops are starting to handle them on a more regular basis. If your local pet shop or reptile dealer does not stock them, ask if they can get them for you or put you in touch with a local breeder. Alternatively, you may see an advertisement in your local paper. If someone has managed to breed them, there could be quite a few babies looking for a good home. Wherever you get your snails, make sure that you are given some basic information, including how old they are. A pet shop should provide a care sheet with any animal sold. Any snail offered for sale should be at least as large as a 5p piece. The shell should be a solid, dark brown colour, which shows that it has hardened up after hatching.

Prices for snails depend on size, and start from 50p for a newly-hatched snail to £25 for a very, very large specimen. The average price seems to be about £2.50 for a snail of about 5cm in shell length.

A group of snails will make short work of a juicy apple!

HOUSING

Land snails must be one of the easiest pets for which to find suitable housing. Ranging from plastic propagators to large fancy tanks, there is guaranteed to be something to fit your home and pocket.

Plastic Tanks

Plastic tanks make superb homes for snails. They are easy to clean, have good ventilation and will stay looking good for years. The cheapest homes for snails must be the plastic propagators that you can buy to grow seedlings in. You can purchase them in any hardware shop or garden centre. Prices start at around £4 and go upwards to around £20 depending on size.

The smallest size suitable for two snails is 45cm x 25cm x 25cm. Of course, as with any animal, you must provide as much room as possible. If you want to grow monster snails they will soon grow out of this size of cage.

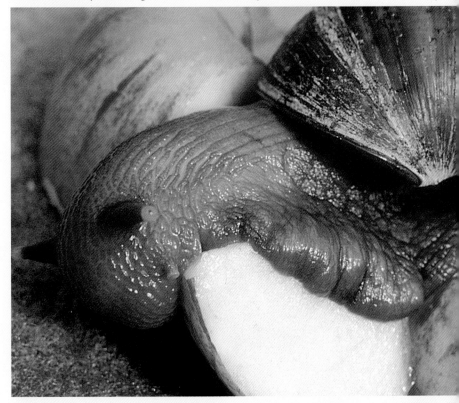

This picture shows clearly how the foot clings to the food while the rasping mouth goes to work.

Above and right: as the snail comes out of its shell, the upper tentacles and eyes unroll until they reach their full length.

The propagator should be in two parts, a coloured base - usually green or brown - and a clear plastic top. Avoid the type made from crushable soft plastic as it won't hold the weight of the snails.

The clear plastic lid should have at least two ventilation panels. Make sure the lid cannot be knocked off by other pets or young children, or you may end up with squashed or eaten snails!

You can also use the clear plastic tanks designed for small mammals and reptiles. These have tight-fitting lids which, if you have a busy household, may be more suitable as snail accommodation. These are easy to clean and the lids provide good ventilation.

Glass Tanks

The cheapest type of glass tank is a second-hand aquarium. Always check there are no sharp edges or cracks in the glass. As the tank will not be holding water it does not have to be watertight. If you ask at your local aquarium or pet shop you may be lucky enough to be given or sold cheaply a leaky or very old tank. After a thorough clean this will make an excellent snail home. Some of the smaller sizes of glass tank come with a plastic lid. Prices for these start from around £8. You can easily make small holes along the back to provide ventilation. You may be able to fix some fine gauge mesh to the lid for even better air circulation.

If your tank does not come with a lid, a condensation tray (which prevents water from evaporating in fish tanks) makes a perfect lid. Again holes can be made and make sure that you find one that fits. A condensation tray costs about £2.50.

Decorative Tanks

Some people like to incorporate their pets into the home by having large, decorative tanks which become a feature in the room. The best one I have ever seen was 90cm x 90cm x 45cm. A wooden frame had been made to match the furniture in the room, and a light was built into the top. Of course this was protected so that the snails did not burn themselves. Snails do not need a light, but this did make the tank look good, and it was easier to see the snails.

Outside the tank at the back was an aquarium background with lots of green plants. Inside the tank were plastic plants (real ones would get eaten) and pieces of bogwood and cork bark. Peat and dried leaves were used on the bottom. The whole effect was stunning, and made a real focal point for the room. There were around ten large snails and hundreds of babies living in total luxury in this tank. Of course not many of us can afford something like this, but use your imagination and add some aquarium background and plastic plants, available from reptile shops, to your own tank and you will be surprised at what you can come up with.

Snails leave a trail of mucus wherever they go. You can see the shine of the mucus at the bottom of this photograph.

Unsuitable Housing

Unsuitable housing for snails are cages made from wire mesh, as these are not comfortable and are difficult to clean. Wooden cages also are not suitable as the snails will eventually eat their way out, and splinters will cause a problem. If you get the opportunity, visit your local zoo and look at how its snails are kept, and see if you can do better.

Temperature

Giant land snails can be kept at a wide range of temperatures, from around 18°C up to 29°C. The higher the temperature the more active the snails will be. The more active they are, the more they will eat and the faster they will grow. This does not mean that you can keep them at low temperatures to save on the food bill! The best temperature for normal growth is about 21-23°C. For most people this is just above normal room temperature. If your house is this warm most of the time then no additional heating is required.

Heating is easy to provide for snails as all they need is gentle background heat to keep them from getting too cold. A small heat mat, the sort designed for reptiles, is available from most pet shops, and it needs to cover only half the tank. The snails will move from the heat mat if they get too warm. You need to switch off the heat in the summer. If the snails stop moving around and disappear into their shells then the tank is too hot or cold. Place a plastic thermometer in the cage so that you can keep a close watch on the temperature.

Substrate

Some people keep their snails in bare tanks, but I do not believe this is the best way to keep snails. Firstly, snails like something to bury themselves in and, secondly, without any substrate to keep the snails odour-free and clean, you will need to clean the tank every day.

I have always found the general-purpose compost sold in garden centres the best material to put in with the snails. From the ecological point of view try and avoid peat, as its removal destroys important natural habitats. Check that no chemicals have been added to the compost or your snails may be poisoned. The compost should cover the bottom of the tank to a depth of about 2cm and kept damp but not soaking wet. Spray the tank lightly with warm water every other day to keep the moisture content at the required level.

Leaf litter and moss can also be placed in the tank, as well as cork bark, all of which provide plenty of places for the snails to hide away. Vermiculite can also be used but nothing works quite as well or is as cheap as compost. Avoid using garden soil which may have pesticides or slug pellets in it and is usually too dry and stony for the snails' liking.

Cleaning Out

As long as your snail tank is not too small, you will only need to clean it out once a week. Do not use any disinfectants or detergents as these may harm your snails. Plain warm water is all you need. Throw away all the old, dirty substrate and replace it with fresh compost. Be sure to wash all the tank or you will get a build-up of mucus which can dry and mark the tank or fungus can grow if the snails are kept too moist. Remember that any decorations must be rinsed as well. As the snails move around you will find a trail of mucus and droppings everywhere. It may be necessary to wipe over the sides of the tank with water during the week, if they get really dirty.

The snail at the front of the photograph is climbing up the glass of its tank.

FEEDING

Inside the snail's mouth is an organ called a *radula*, which contains thousands of 'teeth'. The radula grows continually throughout the life of the snail, and is used to scrape food into the snail's mouth. Watch your snails closely and you will notice that the radula is constantly moving to find food. Snails will happily eat all day, every day.

Feeding Giant African land snails could not be easier. They eat most types of green food happily. The types of greens that snails do best on are leafy green and red lettuce, cabbage, spinach, watercress and normal cress. Snails also eat dandelions and fresh grass. Cucumber and courgette are also taken readily. Any type of fruit is relished, but banana and apple seem to be snail favourites. To ensure your

The snail's eyes are the top pair of tentacles; the bottom pair are sensory organs which the snail uses to find its way around.

snails get a good mixture of food, chop up the green leaves and fruit into small pieces and spread them over the floor of the tank. Snails do not need to eat out of a bowl but, if you find it easier for feeding purposes, you can put the food into a flat saucer.

You will know that you are feeding your snails enough food if they leave the fruit skins and tough bits of vegetable, which are only eaten if food is in short supply.

In zoos, snails get a mixture of oats, calcium and vitamin supplements made into a paste. You could try experimenting, but any food made in this way should be removed after a few hours before it spoils. Some snails will take the pelleted food you can buy for tortoises, which is soaked in water before feeding. It is a good idea to keep some in the cupboard in case you run out of fresh foods. Never feed anything that is not one hundred percent fresh, and remove anything that is not eaten within one day.

The size of the apple in relation to these snails gives a good idea of how big they are.

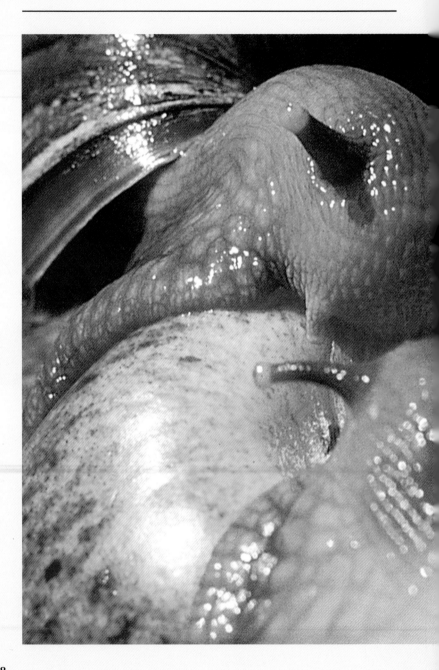

Calcium

The most important part of the snail's diet is calcium. Without this your snail will not be able to make its shell and without its shell it will soon die. Calcium can be given as natural chalk, but the easiest way to provide it is in the form of cuttlefish bone. This is available from any pet shop or, if you live near the beach, see if you can find any washed up on the shore. In this case, do rinse and dry out the cuttlefish bone before giving it to your snail. Calcium can also be given in the form of a powdered supplement sprinkled on the snail's food.

REMEMBER: YOUR SNAIL MUST HAVE A CONSTANT SUPPLY OF CALCIUM

A Liquid Lunch

One of the other things snails like is a drop of beer. They seem to be attracted to the malty, hops flavour. Never offer more than a tablespoonful to an adult snail, and don't give it too often, or you may end up with an alcoholic snail! It does help them grow, so many people give their snails a fortnightly treat of a saucer of beer.

Water

Your snail should be able to get all its water requirements from its food, but keeping a small bowl of water in the cage will not do any harm. The bowl will have to be a heavy one or else it will be overturned. Some snails seem to enjoy drinking, but don't worry if yours ignores the water as it is probably getting its requirements from the food. Never fill the bowl up completely; a few millimetres in the bottom is all that is needed. If you put in any more, the snail might drown.

Spraying the cage with warm water is another good way of providing moisture, as well as keeping the cage conditions at the right humidity.

Getting to know you! During the mating process the snails join their mouth parts, and look as though they are kissing.

Snails are easy to look after and cheap to feed, but are not really affectionate pets!

HEALTH

There is very little that can go wrong with snails. They don't seem to suffer from any specific disease.

Wild snails have a harder time with mites and internal parasites than do their captive relations. In some parts of the world where snails have been introduced they act as an intermediary host for a species of lungworm. This lungworm spends part of its life in the snail, which is then eaten by rodents. The lungworm completes its life cycle and the rodent dies. If you were to eat an affected snail which was not cooked properly, the lungworm would enter your system. It cannot complete its life cycle in humans, but causes cysts within the body and the brain. As you can imagine this creates some problems.

However, the chance of any snail in this country being infected is nil, as they are all captive bred. Also, you would not really wish to eat a raw snail!

The only precaution you need to take with your snails for your safety is to wash your hands after handling them, but this should be done after holding any animal.

There is slight damage to the front of this shell, but it will regrow.

The bottom ring of this snail's shell is new growth which will continue to grow.

A view showing the snail coming out of its shell.

Housing Conditions

Bad housing conditions are most likely to cause any problems. If the tank is too dry the snails will disappear into their shells. Left like this for too long, they may lose too much water, or starve to death while waiting for enough moisture to encourage them to come out of their shells. If your snail does seal itself into its shell through lack of moisture, place it gently in 1.25cm of warm water and the snail will slowly come out of its shell again. Too much moisture will also affect your snail. It may hide away in its shell, but being too wet will kill your snail very quickly. Of course temperature is important; too cold and you may freeze the snail to death, too hot and you will cook it.

Mites

Occasionally you may see tiny mites crawling quickly about the cage and the snails. These do not harm the snails and will not harm you in any way. However, it is not recommended simply to leave them. As snails will be affected by any insecticides, the only treatment is to keep everything as clean as possible and to wash the snails in warm running water every day until all the mites have gone.

Sometimes microworms or grindle worms get into the tank through the food or soil. They do no harm and can be removed by cleaning out the tank thoroughly and replacing the substrate with fresh compost.

Poisoning

It is easier for your snail to be poisoned than you may think. So many things nowadays contain or are treated with pesticide that you must be careful. Wash all food thoroughly before feeding your snails. I have heard of Giant African land snails being poisoned through eating lettuces from supermarkets.

Also be aware that household sprays can affect snails. Fly and flea sprays and powders must be kept well away from your pets. If you can, remove your snails from the room before using these products.

Accidents

Prevention is better than cure, so make sure that the tank is secure and that children and pets cannot get into it or knock it off its base. A little thought now will pay dividends later.

THE SHELL

The shell is the snail's only real defence against predators. It coils in a spiral pattern around a central axis or *columella*. Each whorl gets bigger as the snail grows. At the outermost edge of the shell new 'rings' are formed. The snail makes the outer part of the shell first and then thickens it with special secretions containing calcium carbonate.

Broken Shells

If a snail is dropped, its shell will smash. The amount of damage caused determines whether or not your snail survives. The shell of the Giant African land snail is fairly strong and will survive some knocks without breaking. Any snail that loses a part of its shell will probably die. Some owners have tried to repair the shell but, if it needs artificial repairs, the chances are that the snail has internal injuries and will not survive. Small dents or cracks, however, do not spell the end of your snail. If the snail is fed with extra calcium, it is possible that it can repair its shell by producing new inner layers. This will take quite a long time, so feed a good diet and lots of cuttlefish and, hopefully, you will help your snail to help itself.

The foot of this snail is fully extended out of its shell.

The best course of action is not to let any damage occur in the first place. Follow a few simple rules and you should be all right. Don't handle the snail over a great height, always hold it over a table. Don't leave the snail unattended on a high surface or it could fall off onto the floor where it may get crushed.

Parts Of The Snail

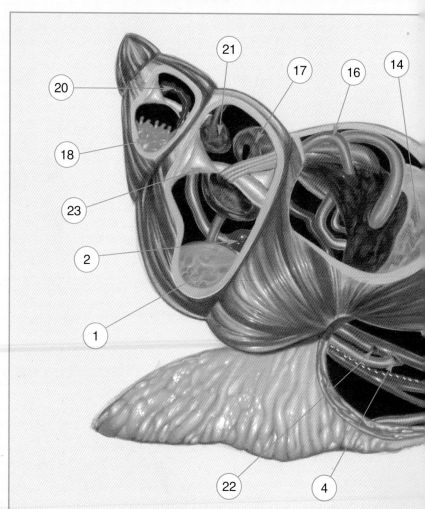

BREEDING

When it comes to reproducing, snails seem to have a very good system. All snails are hermaphrodite. This means they are both male and female. This is very useful for such slow-moving animals.

The Mating Process

Mating in snails is really quite a graceful process. When two snails meet they assess each other to ensure their potential mate is of breeding size. They then touch each

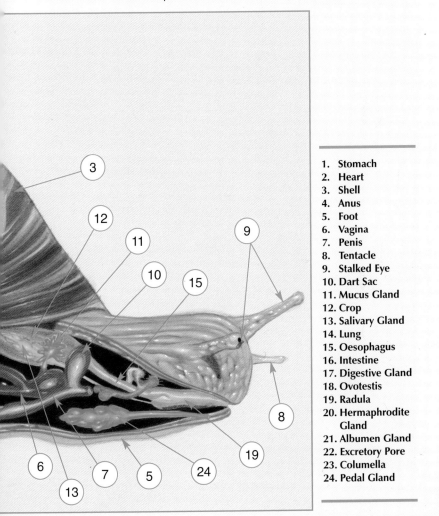

1. Stomach
2. Heart
3. Shell
4. Anus
5. Foot
6. Vagina
7. Penis
8. Tentacle
9. Stalked Eye
10. Dart Sac
11. Mucus Gland
12. Crop
13. Salivary Gland
14. Lung
15. Oesophagus
16. Intestine
17. Digestive Gland
18. Ovotestis
19. Radula
20. Hermaphrodite Gland
21. Albumen Gland
22. Excretory Pore
23. Columella
24. Pedal Gland

other's tentacles. Next the snails slowly rise up on their soles until their mouths are in contact. It makes them look as though they are kissing. After about thirty minutes they lean over and mouth the genitals of the other snail.

Eventually one of the snails will propel a 'love dart' into the body of the other snail. This 'love dart' is made from a chalky substance and seems to be a stimulus

A mixture of eight-week old babies and freshly laid eggs on a wood chipping floor covering.

to breeding. Each snail then joins its genitals with the other. The whole process can take several hours because if the snails cannot match up each other's male and female parts at the same time they start the whole process again. A spermatophore is passed to fertilise the eggs of each snail and mating is complete. The snails can lay several batches of eggs from one mating. The eggs are about 3-4mm and white or pale yellow.

Once the snails start to hatch, the tiny snails can be seen grouping together. The first food they eat is the egg shells. This provides a boost of calcium until they can find more food.

Snails ranging in age from eight weeks to two years, plus freshly laid eggs.

There seems to be no particular time or season when snails mate - they just do it when they feel like it. They must be of a large enough shell size, and 5cm is the smallest I have ever seen mating. The snails have to be of an equal size. The owner of a 12.5cm shell will not fancy a 5cm weakling. Snails use this as a factor in natural selection and to make sure their size and shell strength are always improving.

As long as your snails are roughly the same size, have a good diet and are kept moist and warm it will not be long before you are presented with a batch of eggs. Be careful when you clean out the tank as this is often the first time you will see the eggs. Snails bury their eggs, so this is another good reason to give them a deep substrate. If the eggs dry out they will not hatch.

When you find the eggs place them in a plastic tray - an old margarine tub is

This snail is feeding on small chunks of apple, which is a favourite food of snails.

31

good. The eggs should be moist and warm enough to produce a small amount of condensation on the lid of the box. Most eggs take between a week to two weeks to hatch. At 29°C eggs will hatch within five days.

Problems with hatching can be caused by the eggs being too wet or too dry, or by the parent snails not being in good condition, having a poor diet or not being warm enough.

Once the snails start to hatch, the tiny snails can be seen grouping together. The

This snail has a variety of food in its cage, which will help it to stay healthy.

first food they eat is the egg shells. This provides a boost of calcium until they can find more food. Be careful when handling them at this size as their shells are thin and can be crushed easily. There are two easy ways to move them: either place a whole leaf in the tray and, once all the snails are eating it, move them to a bigger tank, or put their tray inside the new cage and let them glide into the cage.

You can leave the eggs in the main tank to hatch if you like, but this can pose problems in cleaning and the adult snails will disturb the eggs when burrowing. Adult snails will also eat the eggs, so it is preferable if you can move the eggs to safety. Once the babies have hatched and are a few days old they can go in with the adult snails safely.

You will always lose a certain percentage of babies; maybe one in 15 to 20 will not make it, but this is compensated by the sheer volume. The largest number of eggs laid by one of my snails is 229! Most of the time snails will lay their eggs together so it may seem that an individual has laid hundreds when in fact it was the work of two or three snails. If you try to record how many eggs your snails lay and when, you may find patterns emerging and possible triggers for breeding.

Finding Homes For The Babies

Although at first it is very exciting to have all these eggs hatching and watching the babies grow, you will need to find homes for the young snails. Don't let them go anywhere until they are the size of a five pence piece at least. You will always find at least one friend who would like to try to keep snails but this will not solve the problem of disposing of hundreds of babies. Try advertising them in local papers and shops. See if your pet shop would like to take some, and you might even get paid for them! School biology departments are often grateful for donations, and junior or infant schools may fancy some as the class pets.

However you find homes for them, don't expect to make a fortune or to find new homes for all of them in one go. It may take some time.

The Future

Snail ownership can lead to many new friendships. Why not search out other snail owners through your local reptile club or pet club. Some clubs hold snail races - slow but fun!

You will be surprised how many people are interested in snails and other slimy, crawly things. You may be able to help other people with their snails and share your knowledge. Finally, you will be one of those people who will help the Giant African land snail gain its rightful place as an animal worth keeping as a pet.

ACKNOWLEDGEMENTS

The author and the publisher would like to thank the following for their help:
Louise Curtis
Department of Entomology, Natural History Museum,
Invertebrate House, London Zoological Society
Poole Aquarium
Susan Burt

Further titles in the series